PUBLICATION: Absolute Books
                Suite #428
                Private Bag X1
                MELKBOSSTRAND
                7437
                South Africa

EMAIL: info@TheRhinoFoundation.org
              Books@TheRhinoFoundation.org

FIRST PRINT: May 2012
ISBN: 978-0-620-53312-6

© Copyright

*"Fictitious names are used for the Investigation
Officer as well as the blind man and lady who fetched
the bird."*

INTRODUCTION

Fairy Glen Game Reserve is a Big5 Reserve situated in the Brandwacht Mountains close to the Boland town of Worcester, approximately 120km from Cape Town. (South Africa).

This private Reserve consists mostly of fynbos and grass fields and has been in the possession of the De Jager family since the early 1970's. In the year 2000 the Reserve opened its doors to the public for the first time and became famous for the re-location of the *Big5* **of which the Rhino is one.**

According to historical statistics, Simon van der Stel, the last Commander and the first Governor of the Cape during 1691, shot and killed a rhino on this Game Reserve and apparently it was the **last of the white rhino in this region.**

1

Rhinos used to roam freely around Table Mountain at Cape Town (one of the world's seven nature wonders) and the **last rhino was shot in 1853 near Port Elizabeth, approximately 700km North-East from Cape Town.**

ONLY 5 RHINOCEROS SPECIES SURVIVED IN THE WORLD:

WHITE RHINO: Currently only 18 000 survived and is found in Africa.

BLACK RHINO: Only 4 200 survived and is found in Africa.

ONE-HORN RHINO: A rare 2 800 survived and is found in India and Nepal.

JAVAN: The small amount of between 27 and 44 survived and is found in Indonesia.

SUMATRAN: Just 12 to 25 survived and are found in Malaysia.

A FEW IMPORTANT FACTS YOU MIGHT NOT KNOW ABOUT THE RHINOCEROS:

A group of rhinos is called a "crash"

White rhinos aren't white and black rhinos aren't black. The white rhino's name is taken from the Afrikaans word describing its mouth: "wyd", meaning "wide". Early English settlers in South Africa misinterpreted the "wide" for "white".

Rhinos are fast and can run up to 55km per hour, which may not sound like much, but if one is running straight towards you it feels like a *NASCAR* race car is coming your way.

Rhino pregnancies last between 15 to 16 months.

A rhino's skin is much softer than it looks, and is actually quite sensitive to sunburns and insect bites. (That's why rhinos like rolling in the mud so much - it helps to protect them from sunburn and insects.)

The white rhino is the largest rhino (*and the largest land mammal after the elephant*) the bull can weigh from approximately 2000 to 2 300 kg and the cow from about 1 400 to 1 600 kg.

The Sumatran rhino is the smallest rhino, weighing in at a mere 520 to 800 kg.

Rhinos have poor eyesight, but very well developed senses of smell and hearing. (They will charge at you when startled – probably the best way to escape is by climbing a tree, if one is within reach).

African rhinos have symbiotic relationships with Oxpeckers, also called "*tick birds*". In Swahili (an African language), the Oxpecker is called "*askari wa kifaru*", which means "*the rhino's guard*." The Oxpecker eats ticks and insects it finds on the rhino, and creates a commotion when it senses danger.

Most rhinos use piles of dung (*midden*) to leave

5

"messages" for other rhinos - nuances in the smell of dung can tell a rhino a lot about others in the area. **Each rhino's smell identifies its owner as unique** – the smell is different for young vs. adult animals, for males vs. Females, and females in oestro's vs. non-reproductive females. Combined with urine left along trails, dung piles create invisible "borders" around a rhino's territory.

Rhinos have existed on earth for more than 50 million years, and once roamed throughout North-America and Europe (*as well as Asia and Africa*). Throughout their history, rhinos have been a very diverse group. The extinct rhino **Paraceratherium** was the largest land mammal that ever lived, and resembled a big, muscular giraffe. *Telecoeras* was a single-horned, hippo-like grazer common in North America and weighed in the region of 2 300kg.

Three of the 5 surviving rhino species (*one horn, Javan and Sumatran*) are critically endangered.

RHINOPOACHING:

(*MEDIA HIGHLIGHTS!*)

2012-02-29
Sanparks employees caught for poaching: '4 employees of the South African National Parks have been arrested in connection with rhino poaching.' This was confirmed by Sanparks.

2012-02-24
'Seven people were arrested the past week with regards to an International rhino-horn syndicate.'

2012-02-18
'Military technology similar to what has been used in Afghanistan and Mexico can be used in the war against rhino-poachers.'

2012-02-10
'Poachers shoot and kill, rhino cow and her calf at a game Reserve near Letsitele in Limpopo, the police reported.'

THE HISTORY OF HIGGINS AND LADY (WHITE RHINOS)

My intense passion for the **conservation of the white rhino** in this area and to re-establish living members of this specie **specifically at the Reserve**, made me want to fight the dwindling of the rhino population.

In the year 2005 a four-year-old white rhino-bull was bought from Thabazimbi next to the Botswana border and was brought to safety with great care under the professional supervision of a female Veterinary Doctor, 1 500 km to **Fairy Glen Game Reserve**.

The administration involved in authorising the necessary permits from the different institutes and provinces was very hard to do and because of this, we decided to name the rhino-bull after the person who authorised our permit. From there he was called *"Higgins"*.

Higgins adapted incredibly fast and showed his need for a mate during 2010 when it was decided to buy a 5 year-old white rhino cow and soon, the two were inseparable.

Since the beginning, they were as if they were one, slept together at night, walked together all over during the day and Higgins even showed me once how to reproduce in nature, from there she was called *"Lady"*.

Higgins and Lady are the **2 most Southern rhinos in Africa** and cannot speak for themselves. Today I would like to tell the world their **story of pain, love, sadness** and the **extremely strong will to survive** after poachers **butchered them alive and left them to die!**

"Man cannot create. He cannot even re-create that which he has destroyed. He can only conserve." (Rocco Knobel).

11 DECEMBER 2011

"Am I dreaming or playing in a movie without a camera?"

Suddenly, I get shocked back to reality with the smell of fresh blood and a sight that will haunt me for the rest of my life!

It's Sunday morning, my cell phone rings shortly after 07h00. "Who's calling this early?" I ask myself and answer immediately seeing that it must be urgent. Jan, our manager at the Reserve screams frantically, "Pieter, **Lady was poached!**" He seems to have difficulty breathing. My Diesel vehicle cannot drive the 9km to the Reserve quick enough and while driving, I contact the Police, the Vet and a dependable friend, Johan Botma ("Bottie") from my cell phone. My heart is racing, the reality hasn't sunk in and as I drive I pray, "Please God let this be a dream!"Tearing myself up on the inside, I imagine arriving at the Reserve with everything proceeding as normal, I think back to the previous day.

Yesterday, the 10th of December was my son, Pieter's 7th birthday and we had his party at the Reserve.

My daughter Chanelle had chicken-pox and unfortunately had to stay home.

At sunset we watched the **loving couple** lying close to one another next to the waterhole. Higgins always protective over Lady was as relaxed as she was. My peaceful, precious girl, Lady, happy and loved no name could suit her better. Higgins, strong, masculine like a soldier ready to fight any battle, that's how I see him. I sometimes wonder who was more protective over her, Higgins or myself? Knowing their day was close to end with the sun being dipped waist deep in the horizon. Not knowing however, how dark will attack.

My vehicle is still full of balloons and my heart beats in my throat as I reach the gruesome scene. **It breaks my heart and all of a sudden I'm**

terribly nauseous.

With two legs in the air, Lady lies on her side. Chantelle, a lady game-ranger **falls to her knees and cries bitterly** while talking to Lady. **"Please Lady, don't die,"** she says, while wiping out Lady's nose all the time to assist her with her breathing. Her breathing is terribly weak and irregular. Both her horns were butchered out deep into the sinus passages.

I'm stunned, standing next to her, the inside of my sunglasses damp. Realizing how lucky I am that Lady is alive at all, but knowing we have to act fast to keep it this way.

With a huge sigh of relief, I see Bottie arriving and before I can speak to him, he shouts **"where is Higgins**, the bull?!" From a distance I notice 2 game rangers busy searching for Higgins. **I hope and pray that they find him, but at the same time I fear for what we might stumble upon.**

It's Sunday morning and the Vet lives far. My head is spinning and I wonder where I can find an antidote for Lady. By this time I'm positive that she was overdosed with a dart gun containing the **deadly anesthetic drug, M99.**

If she's not going to receive treatment within the next few minutes, **she is going to die**. I can't bear the thought of losing her. In the meantime Jan brings water to keep Lady wet and covers her eyes with a damp cloth to protect it from drying out in the deadly sun rays.

"Bottie, what are we going to do my friend?", I ask, my heart still pounding as I know time is running out. He reacts to what seemed like the answer hit him in the face. "I'll go to a local hospital for help, **we'll have to try a human antidote**. I'll get down on my knees if I have to, there is no other way!" he shouts over his shoulder while running to his pick-up as fast as he can. Clenching my fists I stand and wait..." **are we going to get help, or is Lady going to die?"** Where is Higgins?

13

"Please Lord, let him be alive!" *I send my pleading prayer up above.*

The longest 15 minutes of my life has passed when I suddenly see Bottie with a bag in hand, running from his vehicle towards me. **It is the human antidote known as "Narcan".** The question remains "Is it going to work on Lady?" **An enormous dosage is needed.**

The ear is the only suitable place for me to inject. If she lies on her side any longer, she will damage her organs. We wait, anticipating what will happen? Her ears begin to move. **"Thank Heaven!", she reacts and her breathing sounds better, the reaction brings a cloud of relief over everyone standing by.** From afar I hear a game ranger screaming "here's Higgins!" He is, just like Lady, butchered and critical. He struggles tremendously to breathe. Both his sinus holes are totally open with blood and bubbles oozing from it at the same time. The Vet arrives just in time and immediately tends to Higgins. **"We'll** have to get Stockholm-tar so that we can seal his wounds with it," he says. The local agricultural store is closed and the closest now is Cape Town, which is too far and time is of the essence.

As I lose patience, a Vet who has just about enough tar for Higgins, phones. In the meantime Higgins get treated and injected with antibiotics, vitamins, painkiller, fly-poison and the veterinary antidote M5050. When he reacts, I feel relieve as though a mountain has been lifted from my shoulders. "Just keep Higgins wet!". Bottie shouts over my shoulder. I'm still an emotional wreck as I keep thinking how my rhino-kids will never be the same again. Higgins won't even be able to protect his lady.

SUDDENLY the scene becomes a nightmare. The Police-General, a Senior member of the Department of Nature Conservation, officers of the " Hawks" (a specialized crime unit), a Forensic team, the Media and the detective branch, who's officer in charge demanded that the area be cordoned off, to prevent important evidence from disappearing.

"They won't make it" I hear a random negative person say. It makes my temperature rise on the spot. "I'll show you" I think to myself. Everybody is talking to each other, asking questions and giving their own perspectives. While I, who actually laid the charge and is possibly the most important person at this stage, **gets ignored totally.**

Weakly, Lady gets up and I instantly see the two darts which is still in her left-side. This is what almost killed my girl. I wanted to cradle her, comfort her and tell her everything will be ok. Knowing it's impossible to even wrap my arms around this big animal, I let go of the thought there. A Game-ranger puts on gloves and removes the darts for forensic evidence as a **Captain** of the "Hawks" takes my affidavit and introduces me to the investigating-officer, **which is a constable at this stage.**

"Why do you appoint the **lowest possible rank to investigate such a high profile case?**" I ask, red under my collar, to one of the Senior Officers. "Relax, Mr. de Jager, we will assist her where necessary", he replies. Now, I'm upset! My fists clenched in fury, "do you realise whom you're dealing with? **I am Higgins and Lady's father and trusting friend, be careful!"**

The sun set and **I realise that I cannot leave my two "children" in the bush in this condition and decide to stay with them for monitoring purposes.**

The darkness pours out an old duffle bag of night-sounds.　Suddenly I hear something and immediately wonder where it's coming from?　My heart is pounding and I start sweating profusely.　"What can it be?"　I wonder.　With a sigh of relief I see my friend Bottie pushing a bush to the side so he could pass by.　"Pieter, you haven't eaten anything today!" and passes a sandwich and lovely strong coffee my way.

Exhausted and still stunned, we discuss the episode. "Pieter, do you realise that it was **full moon last night?**" Bottie, who looks like I feel at this stage, asks. "Yes, they call it **Poachers Moon**" I anwser and realise with another shock, what it means.

I look up to the moon which only shows half of his face tonight, **mourning with us**. The Trackers found the trail that leads out of the Reserve in a South-Westerly direction. They cut the electrical fence wiring on that side but the question is: "Where did they enter?" Bottie asks. There are so many unanswered questions now and by midnight Bottie decides to go home.

I lay against a Black Wattle tree, facing the ditch where Higgins was still trapped. I talk to him as if he understands me and says: "**Higgins**, (I whisper) **you cannot leave Lady alone now!**" His ears move independently. He hears me! and for the **first time** in my life **I hear a rhino cry. A sound I cannot describe.** My heart feels as if it wants to **tear**

apart and **I wipe away a tear that runs down my cheek spontaneously.** Through all the other night-sounds, my over-tired body eventually succumbs to sleep.

IT'S MONDAY, day 2

The sun is hot and Lady's condition **deteriorates drastically.** She is busy dehydrating and went to lie down. Since the attack, she didn't eat or drink anything yet. Her wound attracts blowflies which is terribly dangerous, if they lay eggs in her wound, **the maggots could kill her.**

Higgins hasn't eaten either and I still have to keep him wet. At least he managed to move a little today, but not enough to get him out of the ditch.

In the meantime the episode causes havoc right around the world. Radio-stations, newspapers, television-channels as well as Facebook messages reaches me from everywhere. My cell phone works overtime and to prevent any misunderstandings, I decide to handle all the calls myself. An elderly woman from Worcester calls, sobbing she gives her condolences, I do not even know her. A Lady from Stilbaai, Mary-Anne, sends text messages and prayers. From all round the world, people are shocked and furious about the attack on the **innocent Higgins and Lady**. All of a sudden I realise for the first time what a great responsibility I have.

Bottie headed home, while **I decide to spend another night in the bush with my "children."** Luckily he brought me a camping bed and I rest my weary body on it. **The past two days' happenings eat away at my soul and body.** I look up at the Auden Mountain behind me. The mountain, once overtaken by eucalyptus and botanical forest, had burnt the day before the attack and I cannot help but wonder whether it had anything to do with this cruel deed. The neighbour said it was arson. Two helicopters from "Work with Fire" and several staff-members as well as vehicles of the Reserve struggled all day to put out the fire. My mind works overtime! The Reserve's landline was also damaged for how many times and the telephone company just cannot get it fixed. **Can it be related?** Tired of struggling with my thoughts, I turn to Higgins in the ditch.

"You and Lady are my first priority now", I whisper to him. Again, he turns his ears and instinctively I know he heard me.

TUESDAY, day 3

The extreme temperature (38 degrees Celsius) causes Higgins and Lady to dehydrate terribly and if this keeps happening, they will not make it!

The Reserve has a winter rainfall - in summer it is very dry and immensely hot. The rain term from April until August has passed and it **genuinely feels like we are living in the desert.**

Once again I try to put out the water buckets but to no avail. **At this stage both rhinos are so weak that they cannot even lift their heads to drink anymore**. What now?

The white rhino's spine curves downwards from the neck which makes it impossible for them to lift their heads up high. That causes them to eat and drink from the ground.

Bottie builds small flat pools, but without success. "Just don't lose faith and give up Pieter!" Bottie encourages me. "I have never," I think to myself. What worries me is how they cope without one another.

All of a sudden the most **amazing thing happens** and I feel **how our Creator** answers everybody's prayers! **The clouds start to gather and it does not only become cool, but cold and rain follows with snow,** (which is unheard of during December months in Worcester) on the Brandwacht Mountains.

I give a sigh of relief as I realise that Higgins and Lady have been given a second chance on survival. **Amazingly, they start to drink the puddles of water in front of them.** We're all stunned and realise that now there is no turning back. **They will definitely survive!**

To my embarrassment, I feel my long beard and get the smell of bush on my body and clothing. I get the picture of a mongoose in my mind which is self-explanatory, because I'm sure that by this time I must smell like one, but I haven't been home in 3 days.

Two shiny eyes peep at me as I try to get some sleep, it's a little grey buck who gets the biggest shock when it notices me. I'm wide awake again and can't sleep.

Are the people totally out of their minds? **The horn is made of keratin**, the same material that **hair** and **nails in humans** are made of. Where will they be getting the dart-guns and anaesthetics to which **only Veterinary doctors have access?** How are we ever going to stop these unnecessary deeds and useless urges that cause so much pain and suffering?

Once again I realise that Higgins and Lady are of the very few survivors that ever bridged such a terrible ordeal. *During 2011 there were more than 450 deaths reported due to poaching of rhinos.* They are my first priority now. I whisper to Higgins again and dose off.

WEDNESDAY, day 4

It's just after the first light and **the weather is still cool.** Both Higgins and Lady **show definite improval.**

I sit in the shade of a nearby bush and see that Higgins is starting to move more actively. He starts making the weirdest sounds and I instinctively realise **that it's his emergency calls to Lady.**

I move slowly towards him and watch while he amazingly struggles out of the ditch by himself. At first he looks confused, as if he does not know which route to choose. He starts to walk ... but in the wrong direction heading straight towards the lions' spot. He keeps on bashing into the bushes, and struggles over his feet.

Shocked, I realise that he might be blinded as a result of the tremendous trauma and the ultra

26

violet rays or that he might be disorientated without his horns.

I respect the distance between us, but still follow him up to where he lies, close to the area where the lions are located.

My cell phone rings and I know the voice very well. "Pieter, **I have information**", it comes from a professional friend. I'm stunned and search nervously for my diary to write down what he has to say.

Names of suspects, as well as a description of the **alleged vehicle** used during the attack, is given to me, and **where the horns might possibly be hidden**. Time is running out and we'll have to move fast before the suspects move the horns or flee. I am nervous and while shaking like a leaf, my trembling fingers search for the Colonel's cell number. With my second try, the number rings correctly. "I'm busy with an investigation in Cape Town" he says, but will see that the Investigating-Officer (constable) will **report** to you **by 07h30 tomorrow**.

I walk up and down. We are working with **syndicates, emotionless criminals!** An International television-team visits me for an interview regarding the gruesome attack. I struggle to concentrate on the interview, my mind stays with the Investigating-Officer and the suspects. Everything gets too much for me now and it feels like my head want to burst, but I won't give up.

Luckily my "children" are drinking the water and I don't have to worry about them dehydrating anymore. It worries me that they haven't eaten anything yet, although **they can stay without food for quite some time because of the healthy condition which they were in before the attack.**

I am so content that I can actually go and sleep at home tonight. The rhinos are two kilometres apart from one another and Higgins is safely out of the ditch. There won't be any sense in sleeping in the bush again tonight. The game-rangers have strict scheduled times to visit the bush however.

My hope is with the Police and with them in my head I eat, drink and sleep tonight.

THURSDAY, day 5

It is early morning and already terribly hot as I enter the Reserve. As always, Bottie is there with a flask of coffee and sandwiches. I notice that he has the local newspaper (Worcester Standard) with him and hands it to me. "Page one until three are full of news regarding the rhinos and the Reserve", he says.

"This, the other animals won't smell and we must make Higgins and Lady eat today", says Bottie while pointing to a bale of hay at the back of his pick-up. In the meantime the Police stay on my mind.

"When will the Police arrive?" Bottie and I start our search for Higgins. Bottie is first to notice him at the Audens Mountain side. We throw the bale of hay off the vehicle and wait patiently to see whether Higgins will eat. He tastes slowly, and wonderfully eats half of it quite easily. We

30

continue our search for Lady and strangely enough we find her on the western side of the Reserve. The two of them are usually inseparable and now they seem to be on two complete opposite sides of the Reserve, which doesn't make sense at all. I put the hay alongside a tree for her, but she only smells it and walks away. **She looks so sad and, with great difficulty, I swallow the lump in my throat.**

By sunset I realise that I have not heard from the Police at all and upset and disappointed in them, **I wonder how trustworthy this service is.**

I once again feel safe to sleep at home tonight and decide to take matter in my own hands and make use of my own contacts. I manage to get the number of a more senior person, also a Colonel, from a secret agent. **Utterly angry and upset, I contact him telephonically.** "Sir, please calm down!" it comes from an astonished Colonel. "I don't know what you're talking about!" Physically and emotionally drained, I sit down and start to explain in better language to him what my problem is with the Police's Investigating Officer. "Talk to the Colonel of the department!" he says. "Are you insane?" I ask. "I want nothing to do with him or the constable!"by now I'm shouting.

Approximately fifteen minutes later Officer Fritz from the Hawks phones me. Immediately I get a calm feeling that I am now dealing with the right person and we make an appointment for 09h00 the next morning.

It's Friday as well as a Public Holiday - I'm not at all surprised to find that it's the Investigating Officer Mr Fritz, is 30 minutes early with his call. We meet at the Lodge at Fairy Glen.

While I ask him more about his background, I realise that I am dealing with the ideal person now. He comes from Johannesburg where he used to work in Brixton at the Murder and Robbery unit. While we chat, I find that, as an ex police-officer,

I feel safe now.   All the information is given to him and he departs for his investigation. The grin on my face is obvious when I see a packed suitcase in the back of his vehicle, I just know this man is ideal for the job, **although we cannot make up for lost time.**

I'm still thinking of a plan to make Lady eat. **Maybe I should bribe her with molasses. It has a sweet, sugar smell and gives instant energy.** Exactly what she needs!

She moved in a Southern direction and stopped when she heard me.   She turns and moves in my direction at a slow pace.   I just know, today is the day! **I put the molasses on top of the hay bale and cannot believe my eyes to what is happening in front of me.   She eats!...but with great difficulty.** I slowly move closer and realise that she has **a massive cut in her upper-lip. The bastards! They missed her horn and cut her lip instead.**   She struggles, but eats a little bit.

I answer my phone which rings non-stop. It's my cousin Bennie, from Pretoria. He reminds me that I must fetch him and his family from the airport on Sunday. I totally forgot about that! We arranged a holiday at the East Coast months ago. What am I to do? Bennie is on his way, but **I cannot leave the rhinos like this.**

The one radio-station after the other interviewed me already. Several *TV-channels* as far as *China, France and Germany* were at the Reserve this week.

I'm literally exhausted and decide to take some energy medication to help me through this trial period.

Things are taking a nasty turn again as Higgins walks in circles. His immunity is too low to give him more anaesthetic so that we can determine what the problem is. How close do I dare get to him? I zoom into his eyes with my camera. It looks like cataracts or is it his eye lenses that are damaged? **Lenses will be a tremendous**

problem, because **help will have to be flown in from abroad.** All the **signs that Higgins is totally blind are clear.** As he lies down it gives me the perfect opportunity to spray for blowflies but what next?

It is Sunday and as usual my friend Bottie is by my side. Without him we would be lost. Luckily I have some time to fetch my cousin at the airport, but before that happens, I have to make sure that I can dare to leave Higgins and Lady behind on the Reserve. Searching, I go through the Reserve until I find Higgins where he is lying in a shallow mud-pool. **Terrified,** I see that **Letaba,** one of the **large elephant-bulls is approaching Higgins** and standing approximately 10 meters from where he is. Letaba slowly approaches Higgins and **reaches out to him with his trunk.** I get all tensed up and, with my breath held up, expect the worst, but after a few minutes which felt like hours, Letaba turns around and walks away peacefully. I realise at once that he **made peace with the terrible state Higgins is in.**

Fortunately, my cousin and his family are at ease with my situation, and understand the circumstances. They are happy to spend their first week of the holiday at the Reserve. Bennie assists me in the field around every possible corner with Higgins and Lady's recovering-program.

Today, I get caught off guard when my friend Andrew, phones from Cape Town. "What's going on?" he asks. Cape Town is full of pamphlets saying that **Higgins and Lady must be put out of their misery** because of **their pain and suffering.** I am horrified by what I am hearing and before I can grasp this entirely, my phone rings again. It's a lady from a Cape Town morning newspaper.

"A Journalist forwarded an article to us stating that the rhinos are not being respected, suffering tremendously and **should be put down**." What nonsense is this? I think to myself and ask the lady to forward the email to me. With a shock I realise that it is "Anne" who visited the rhinos a few days ago and has forwarded an email to me where she thanked me for all my efforts and positive work concerning the rhinos. Now I don't understand at all! **She is looking for cheap sensation,** but the article however still gets published in the newspapers, the SPCA (animal welfare) visits me as well. The SPCA is very impressed with the progress and treatment of both Higgins and Lady.

TUESDAY, 20 DECEMBER
"CALL FOR INJURED ANIMALS TO BE PUT DOWN"

appears in a Cape Town morning newspaper. What else? **Now the public is furious** and this helps me through a tremendously trying time. The same newspaper phones me again and asks if I'm aware that the Police tracked down a store in Cape Town where they found rhino-horns as well as elephant tusks. Two Chinese men were arrested. I get the address and contact the Investigating Officer, Mr. Fritz, with the information. Stressed, I await follow-up and receive the disappointing news that only Ivory elephant tusks were found.

WEDNESDAY, 21 DECEMBER

Enough is enough! I am putting my foot down right here. **Higgins, Lady and I are going to get through this,** with or without negative publicity.

Higgins's sight has improved slightly and he does not walk in circles anymore.

After all the moaning and groaning of my friend Bottie and my family, I decide to take a break after all. I cannot be of any use to Higgins and Lady the way I felt recently, overworked and exhausted. Luckily, Bottie reassures me that he will take my place and that he will report back to me on a daily basis with the rhinos' development. We pack the Kombi and take the road to the East Coast with Higgins and Lady still in my system. **"Am I making the right decision?"**
My phone is constantly ringing, news agencies and radio-stations calling and at the same time

Bottie keeps me updated at least 3 times a day telephonically.

Only on Christmas Day, my family and I could sit around the campfire peacefully without being disturbed. Bennie tries to cheer me up with a delicious meal and helicopter-ride in Knysna, but my mind is with my "children" on the Reserve. **What if something goes wrong?**

We all get excited when we decide to take an afternoon trip on a racing boat, but that all changes suddenly after an **unexpected phone call.**

It's Mike, *a blind man working in Export.* He says his life is in danger and that he wants to talk. He sounds very convincing. To top it all, my son, Pieter gets Chicken-pox and gives us all the more reason to pack and return home. While we're busy packing, I receive another call from Mike and he asks whether I'm prepared to take a parcel with us to Worcester, which will only be delivered to me the next morning at 07h00. **Suddenly, I feel unsafe!** Am I scratching too deeply into the criminals' activities that they want me out of the way? I wake up early in the morning and drive down to the security gates of the holiday residence. Uneasily, I wait for "somebody" to arrive.

After approximately 10 minutes a vehicle arrives, parks within a distance and an elderly lady who calls herself "Suzy", appears and introduces herself to me. I try to see what the registration number of the vehicle is, but to no avail. Astonished, I stand watching as she takes out a cage with a parrot and hands it to me. "Will this be the parcel that must go to Worcester?" Naively I try to talk to the parrot, but it does not respond.

On my journey returning home, my phone rings. Inquisitively I try to see **who it is, but no number appears on my screen. I answer and the man speaking threatens me in a perfect English accent. "Careful!!!, you're playing with fire** and you are going to burn your fingers!" **"You don't frighten me!"** I answered and am now more determined than ever to get to the Reserve as soon as possible. I'm petrified something might happen to Higgins and Lady again.

As soon as we arrive in Worcester, an unknown woman arranges to come fetch the parrot from me. She has a message from Mike who asks if we can meet the next morning at 11h00.

The time for the meeting has arrived, and at exactly 11h00 the Investigation Officer, Mr. Fritz and I knock at the discussed address. **The blind man nervously opens the door** and invites us inside. We sit down and wait anxiously on the promised information. He sits opposite us and **removes**, what he calls, two **plastic eyes** in front of us. **"My eyes have already been removed because I saw too much!"**, he says. A cold chill runs down my spine as I turned to Mr. Fritz. "Look!" says the blind man and shows us his forearms of which both wrists has been cut. "The nerves are so damaged that I have no feeling in my finger points and as a result of that, I can also not read Braille, the blind language" he says.

His right arm was also **chopped away with a machete**, he shows us.

"Please stay calm and trust us, you're safe," I try to calm Mike who keeps on telling us that he feels unsafe. Mike's hell started when he advertised for a partner in business on the Internet. He is the **owner** of an **Import and Export Company** in Cape Town. **"My new partner was a Chinese"** and he starts opening up towards us. **"I was previously used by the Police"**, and start giving us names of the Police Officers which we make notes of. "I do not trust the Police!", he says. Trust me then, it's my rhinos that have been poached! "Yes, I know, I heard on the news. I also touched a rhino horn last week that had to be exported!" How do you know if you do not have feeling in your finger points?" I ask suspiciously. "And how do you know when it's genuine?", Mr. Fritz asks. "I can smell it and know from the rough texture", he explains while sitting on the edge of his chair. The atmosphere in the room stays very tense and the lady who fetched the parrot from me appears in the doorway. "Do you want to drink anything?"she asks politely and it's only Mike who decides to have a cup of tea. **"I will do the deal,"** it comes from Mike who appears to be very uncomfortable, "but I want Police clearance and that they will guarantee to protect me." This guarantee is not so easy to get hold of, as it sounds, explains Mr. Fritz worringly. "Well, then I'm not going to put my life at stake anymore to work with you!", it comes from Mike. **Is this man playing a game that can endanger my life...?** Is he maybe **on the side of the criminals?**

My investigation with the blind man comes to an end. I feel miserable and want to give up, but I cannot do that. I made a promise that I will get these cruel and evil monsters who did this, catch them and make them pay.

I subsequently get very ill and am confined to bed. Can it be? At my age I get Chicken Pox. It makes me incredibly ill and I have to stay in bed and at home for two weeks according to Drs orders. Luckily my very reliable friend Bottie is with Higgins and Lady every day and I know they are in good hands.

After three days at home I get yet another telephone call from Jan, manager at the Game Reserve, telling me that **the Reserve is burning profusely.** "Helicopters are on their way to help stop the fire", he says. Immediately I jump out of bed and know that I'm doing the wrong thing now, because the Doctor told me that sunlight is very bad, but feel I have no other choice. My Diesel vehicle is once again too slow to reach the Reserve in time and from a distance I can see the **flames and billowing dark clouds of smoke.** Glowing emergency lights and sirens can be heard. My biggest worry is

the rhinos, **especially Higgins**, because his sight is very poor and if he gets to close to the fire, **the smoke and flames can overpower him.**

Again, **it's a hectic scene that awaits me.** Four helicopters start to circle around the Reserve and the **animals are bewildered and scattered all over.** "What are you doing? Look at you, you're playing with your life!," Bottie shouts at me from behind. **"We must find Higgins and Lady,** where are they?", I answer.

My nerves are shattered! "Lady is safe!", he calms me, but my biggest concern is Higgins. Bottie has already arranged with the pilots of the helicopters to look out for him. "He is at the big Dam where the helicopters get their water from", it comes via Bottie's radio. **That is not good news at all,** because Higgins can run into the dam and drown. If the helicopters stop to scoop water the chalets and the Lodge can burn down as well. Suddenly I see how Higgins runs up and down and **falls over his feet.** "Good Heavens, Bottie, what are you doing?" I shout over the noise when I see him walking straight towards Higgins. "Don't worry, he let me get close to him before", he tries to assure me. I turn ice cold when he goes straight up to Higgins and talks to him. Higgins's ears turn again like when I spoke to him. **Higgins also started to**

trust Bottie during this time. It speaks for itself when I notice how Higgins follows Bottie away from the noise at the dam. **I cannot believe my eyes! Once again, the Lord above made me aware that wonders will never cease** and I can return to my sickbed. Higgins and Lady are safe!

The Chicken Pox heals too slow to my liking and I find myself slipping away from home like a naughty teenager, to visit Higgins and Lady to see if they are safe. Everytime I find Bottie, out of free will, on his post. Bottie and I hold a quick meeting while I'm still in bed. **We come to the conclusion that it's both our dream and desire that Higgins and Lady get together again.**

They have been through so much danger, pain and suffering and still they survive! "Bottie, I saw how Higgins followed you at the dam, can't we try that to see whether he finds Lady?", I suggest. I decide there and then to make my recovering date earlier and together

Bottie and I go into the field on Monday morning.

Higgins's wound is extremely red, because he keeps on walking into the trees and bushes as a result of his poor vision. We spray for flies again and Bottie starts talking to Higgins in a soft tone of voice while holding lucerne out to him. **It works and slowly Higgins follows Bottie.** It's a long stretch and Higgins and Bottie walk slowly while I drive behind them with the pick-up. It is already 14h00 and we've been in the field for 5 hours. **Bottie is burnt red from the sun and his feet are terribly painful when Higgins suddenly comes to a halt! He turns his head to the left, smells in the air and starts to call which we can only assume is for Lady.** We suddenly see her running out of the bushes towards him.

LADY AND HIGGINS MEET EACH OTHER IN THE MIDDLE OF THE ROAD!!!

She literally kisses him and **I struggle to hold back the tears!** Lady takes the lead and Higgins follows her due to the fact that he struggles with his eyesight.

The couple is so happy! It feels like a dream, or even better, a movie that is playing right in front of us. Although they will never be normal again. Without horns Higgins and Lady start a new life together and I realise once again that I will fight these criminals till the better end.

There is still a long road to recovery..... I LOVE THEM SO MUCH .....they survived.

(GENESIS 1 VERSE 26): (New International Version)

Then God said, *"Let us make mankind in our image, in our likeness, so that they may rule over the fish in the sea and the birds in the sky, over the livestock and all the wild animals, and over all the creatures that move along the ground."*

Higgins and Lady's auspicious days.

Fire at the Reserve a day before the attack.

Chantelle whilst kneeling over Lady
crying bitterly.

Bottie and I performing the intravenous
treatment Narcan, on Lady.

53

Riaan, a game ranger removes two darts from Lady's side for forensic research.

Lady responds positively to the antidote and yields.

Higgins found in a ditch.

Bottie in the ditch with Higgins.

Dr Bellstead treats Higgins' mutilated face.

The endeavour to imitate a walk out of the ditch for Higgins, collapses.

The badly dehydrated Lady keeps herself
erect between 2 trees to survive.

The condition of Lady deteriorates and
she lies down against a tree.

Higgens in the dam trying to cover
himself with mud.

Letaba walks towards Higgins.

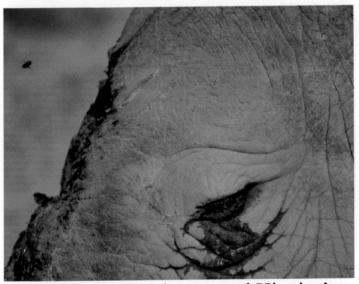

A blow fly revolve around Higgins'
wound trying to lay eggs.

Fire at the Reserve after the attack.

Higgins anxiously runs whilst falling
over his feet at the dam as
helicopters are busy scooping out water
to extinguish the fire.

A dart gun, panga, feather darts and anaesthetic similar to those used in attack.

Higgins and Lady before the reign of terror.

The last photo taken of Higgins before the atrocity.

Higgins and Lady found one another at last!

MY PLEA

It will not be wise to look for the problem from abroad, but rather right here on our own doorsteps.

Proposals to dehorn the rhinos ourselves are unwise. The biggest risk to the rhino is associated with the immobilisation process, which is inherently dangerous and can be fatal. The biggest risk to the rhino owner is being in possession of the very commodity that poachers are after. Keeping of horns, especially in large numbers, exposes the owner to being the victim of potential criminal activity. A number of armed robberies involving the theft of entire stockpiles have already occurred in South Africa. The targets included museums, national parks, taxidermist studios as well as private individuals.

Poachers are prepared to remove any vestige of horns, including the small growth nubs on rhino calves, and therefore dehorning is unlikely to be an adequate deterrant. Legalising will introduce rhino horn to millions more people.

(To spray poison in the horns can lead to another murder weapon at the end of the chain).

Weapons which are used in many of these cruel crimes, are currently sold over the counter. Authorities will need to have this licensed like a firearm seeing that it is just as deadly. Proper control can be practised this way.

Veterinary practitioners must be protected with the use of the product M99 or similar deadly products and must be forced to be present with the use of this product at all times to practise better control.

Stronger control at Customs must be practised. Awareness programmes must be implied across the world and locally and must be financed and lodged through the authorities. Without that we cannot get the message across.

May this life changing experience that I shared with you in this book, be an inspiration to you and may we, together, fight for the survival of these amazing animals and stop the extinction of these species.

Rhino Greetings

PIETER DE JAGER

ACKNOWLEDGEMENTS

Dr Belstead, the Veterinary Practitioner for his incredible passion with which he handled the situation.

Johan Botma "Bottie"who, at least twice a day until the conclusion of this book, monitored Higgins and Lady himself. For the impeccable way he bonded with them and the great impact he had on their recovery.

Tanja for her incredible patience and motivation (behind the scenes) while she had to keep the ball rolling at home on her own. Although her life was also endangered, she kept me positive all the way!

Denis Pothas and Goggy for the incredible world-wide assistance and awareness-programme for Higgins and Lady.

Cathy Holmes for the Internet footage.

Mara Louw for the rhino projects.

Martin Steyn for the DVD footage.

All Game rangers who rotated and worked nightshifts to ensure the safety of Higgins and Lady.

All the hundreds of people with messages and assistance of which ever nature. Without your prayers this miracle would never be possible!

FACTS SUMMARY

- http://www.rhinos-irf.org/25-things/

- http://www.iol.co.za/the-star/poachers-leave-rhinos-hornless-and-in-agony-1.1196340

- http://www.eoearth.org/article/Poaching

- Magela Peter (lead author);

- Sylvio G. Codella, Yahya Eid Ph.D. (Topic Editor) "Poaching".

- In: Encyclopedia of Earth. Eds. Cutler J. Cleveland (Washington, D.C.: Environmental Information Coalition, National Council for Science and the Environment).

- First published in the Encyclopedia of Earth October 5, 2007;

- Last revised date: May 12, 2011;

- Retrieved February 25, 2012: http//www. eoearth.org/article/Poaching.

- Magelah Peter Gwayaka is a social science graduate from Makerere University Kampala (Uganda).

- http//www.savetherhino.org/etargetsrinm/ site/1/default. aspx?gclid=CMbPnNDxuK4CFYsntAo

- http//www.ecotricity.co.uk/ landing/?partner=SR1

- http//www.afrikaans.news24.com/Tags/ Topics.

- Bible Gateway.com Genesis1 Verse 26. (New International Version).